A BETTER BOY

A Better Boy

A Titanic Monologue

John Wilson Foster

Belcouver Press

by the same author

Forces and Themes in Ulster Fiction (1974)
Fictions of the Irish Literary Revival (1987)
Colonial Consequences: Essays in Irish Literature and Culture
(1991)
The Achievement of Seamus Heaney (1995)
Nature in Ireland (ed., 1997)
Titanic (ed., 1999)
Recoveries: Neglected Episodes in Irish Cultural History (2002)
Irish Novels 1890–1940 (2008)
Between Shadows: Modern Irish Writing and Culture (2009)
Titanic: The Sceptre of Power (2016)
Titanic: Culture and Calamity (2016)
Pilgrims of the Air: The Passing of the Passenger Pigeons (2017)

First published in 2017 by Belcouver Press, Portaferry,
Northern Ireland
www.belcouverpress.com

Copyright © 2012, 2017 John Wilson Foster

Cover Cover: Ian McElhinney as Lord Pirrie;
photo by Conleth White

Typeset by CB editions, London
Printed in England by ImprintDigital, Exeter EX5 5HY

ISBN 978-0-9935607-1-2

ACKNOWLEDGEMENTS

I am most grateful to the actors Lalor Roddy (and Kabosh Theatre Company) and Ian McElhinney (and Rathmore Productions) for bringing to life on stage the historical figure, William J. (Lord) Pirrie, whom I merely imagined in the privacy of my study. Ian amidst a busy schedule (including camera calls for *Game of Thrones*) took Pirrie on what for me was an inspiring journey. I am grateful, too, to Damian Smyth not only for his early encouragement but for his engaged responses to the stagings. I am also indebted to the following for their help and encouragement through various stages of composition and production of *A Better Boy*: Noirin McKinney, Gilly Campbell and Robert Stephenson (Arts Council of Northern Ireland); Kenneth Irvine and Esther Haller-Clarke (Aspects Irish Literature Festival, Bangor); Philip Hammond, Dick McKenzie and Ann Doherty (Belfast Titanic Company); Mark Phelan, Ross McDade and Ryan Crown (Brian Friel Theatre, Belfast); Sean Kelly (Cathedral Quarter Arts Festival, Belfast); Nora Hickey M'Sichili, Alexander Zuddas and Rosetta Beaugendre (Centre Culturel Irlandais, Paris); Paula McFetridge (Kabosh Theatre Company); Deborah Douglas (Linen Hall Library); Gerry Mulligan, Johanna Haughey and Corinne Becquevort (Northern Ireland Executive Office, Brussels); Ian Montgomery and Steven Scarth (Public Record Office of Northern Ireland); Conleth White, Lisa-Marie Cooke and Cara McGimpsey (Rathmore Productions creative team); Johanna Leech (Strand Arts Centre, Belfast); Aubrey Irwin, Anne Zemmour and Caoimhe Ní Mhuilleoir (Tourism Ireland); Alex Graham (Ulster Reform Club); Johnny Andrews; Peter Cavanagh, Jo Egan and Richard Jolly. I was delighted (and a touch apprehensive) when members of the Andrews and Pirrie families came to the play; when one evening a small group of Harland & Wolff employees turned up, I was equally delighted.

CONTENTS

A Better Boy was commissioned by the Belfast Titanic Company to observe the centenary of the sinking of RMS *Titanic*. It was first performed on the Barge MV *Confiance*, Lanyon Quay (River Lagan), Belfast on April 9th, 2012. Lalor Roddy took the part of Lord Pirrie and the play was directed by Paula McFetridge of Kabosh Theatre Company. There was a revival of the monologue on December 5th, 2013 in the Brian Friel Theatre (Queen's University, Belfast) in which Ian McElhinney played Pirrie; it was directed by the actor and writer for Rathmore Productions. Thereafter it was performed by Ian McElhinney in Bangor, Belfast, Brussels and Paris.

Application for performance should be made before commencement of rehearsal to Belcouver Press, 44 Shore Road, Portaferry, Northern Ireland BT22 1JZ, United Kingdom.

A Better Boy

1917. Witley Park, Surrey

William J. Pirrie of Conlig, County Down and Quebec, Canada occasionally sits in a not too comfortable chair, since he is always ready for decision and action. At his elbow is a table on which rests a largish notebook which contains his personal journal which he intermittently consults and reads from (in a different font). [*The notebook can contain the text of the monologue and the actor can of course use it as a promptbook if necessary, given the density of the monologue.*] *But Pirrie had always a prodigious memory for detail and so is prepared for any questions he might be asked. In any case, he reckons on talking about more than Tommie Andrews and* Titanic. *It is mid-April 1917, before Pirrie is called upon to take wartime control of British merchant shipping. He has condescended to give an interview in which he will be asked to remember his nephew Tommie Andrews, chief designer of RMS* Titanic, *a ship whose name Pirrie is loath to speak.* (And it requires great vigilance for the word Titanic not to escape his lips.) *Yet he sees an opportunity to give his side of the* Titanic *story under cover of commemorating his nephew. His interviewer is unseen, slightly to the side of the audience. The unheard questions he is asked are few (Pirrie is a celebrated public speaker who enjoys talking) and are implicit in the answers he gives.* [*I have inserted them in square brackets and in italics but they are unspoken. An alert pause can signal their being asked. The effect of Pirrie's first speaking should be that of in media res as though momentum had already been built up.*]

Pirrie is distinguished looking, silver-bearded, and in the ordinary formal dress (suit with waistcoat and fob-watch and chain) used in those days to greet visitors. His trademark yachting cap sits ostentatiously nearby. He is a neat, composed, and for the most part confident figure, though sometimes shows signs of strain. He is, perhaps justifiably, a little conceited, something of the affable martinet. Like many self-made men, he is too impatient to linger in undue sympathy and sentiment. Yet like many successful, 'hardbitten' businessmen, he has sentimental tastes in art and literature. He finds it hard to talk at length about someone other than himself and business: he dwells in the future and not the past (except to recall and savour his accomplishments). As the interview proceeds, fewer questions are asked as it increasingly becomes a monologue. He occasionally brandishes an unlit cigar.

On the table is also a smaller well-thumbed notebook and a couple of magazines (no doubt devoted to shipbuilding). Pirrie is in the 'smoking room' or saloon of Witley Park (Lord Pirrie's Surrey mansion), a glass dome above his head, for astonishingly the room is under the lake in the grounds of his Surrey mansion and carp imported from Azay le Rideau in the Loire Valley can occasionally be seen meandering by. The irony goes unremarked. He gets up occasionally and moves around as the actor desires, making appropriate eye-contact with his unseen interlocutor.

[*The paragraphs in the script are often just for ease of memorisation and not necessarily to signal a change of topic or tone.*]

★

Note to actor: Pirrie speaks in a rather businesslike fashion at first. He begins by lauding Tommie perhaps a trifle dutifully or by enthusiastic rote (with something of the distractedness of the busy man with some current business transaction or obligation of high office also in mind); then steers from the subject into his own passionate view of things, and ends surprised at discovering how much he misses Tommie. To put it another way, he begins with a somewhat faux though vigorous empathy, allows his vanity to show in his deep concern for the achievements of Harland & Wolff and himself, and ends in some humility and genuine sorrow. Pirrie's interview is often an advertisement for himself but becomes a small journey of self-discovery; he begins as Yeats's 'public smiling man' and ends as far more human. If desirable, the magazine he reads Bram Stoker's article from can be on a neighbouring bookshelf, allowing the actor a pretext to get up, walk around, and resume his seat when he wishes.

*

A short selection of contemporary 'hits' can be played in the auditorium before curtain-up. They might include Marion Harris singing 'I Ain't Got Nobody' and 'Beale Street Blues', Count John McCormack singing 'Little Mother of Mine', and the George Lewis Band playing 'Yaaka Hula Hickey Dula'. The music fades and lights go up as the audience discovers Pirrie at a sideboard offering the unseen interviewer a drink (which is declined) and pouring himself a brandy from a decanter into a snifter. If stage layout circumstances require, he can enter talking to the interviewer who follows him, either from the wings or from the auditorium. In any case, he has paused after being asked the first question.

[*How did the people of Belfast respond to the death of Mr Andrews?*]

– Well, they couldn't *believe* he'd gone. The people of Belfast loved my nephew Tommie. The churches were thronged the Sunday after. The roads were black with people after the services, up and down the land. They came to pay their respects to the men from the Yard who'd been on board to guarantee all was shipshape. Grand fellows, some of whom knew the ship from stem to stern – and that was a very long way!

They came to remember everyone, but especially Tommie. I never met the man who had anything but a good word to say about him. At the services grown men could cry in public without embarrassment – and they did. For Tommie must have seemed to them practically un- . . . (*pausing, perhaps to taste – or keep at arm's length – a looming irony, as he almost utters the notorious phrase 'practically unsinkable' that haunted the inquiries*) . . . practically *in*destructible.

And word had obviously got round about Montgomery's cable from New York after he had spoken to survivors on the *Carpathia* (*sign-writing in the air*) – 'All unanimous Andrews heroic unto death'. At least, the Dean of Belfast knew of it, for he quoted it in the Cathedral, I was told. (*Sitting*) I was at here at

Witley, resting. I always travelled on the maiden voyages
– the big ones anyway – but my doctor forbade it. And
Alec Carlisle, our managing director . . . *he* changed his
mind at the last moment and stayed away too. He called
the ship his last baby and then retired. He was distraught
when it . . . died in infancy. He fainted in St Paul's
at the memorial service. (*Pause, recovering, disguising
defensiveness with pride*) We both had a hand in it, the sum
and summit of our achievement in ship design. But we
left it all in dear Tommie's hands.

[*Was Harland & Wolff worried, with you and Mr Carlisle
absent from the maiden voyage?*]

– No, we'd no worries on that score. We'd every
confidence in Tommie. Capable hands. Strong chap.
Never sick. Never missed a day's work through all
his apprenticeship. Though he *was* late *once . . . by ten
minutes!* It became family lore. (*Chuckles*) Got there
at ten past six in the morning and had to hang about
outside the gates on Queen's Road til they let him in at
breakfast-time. Other young fellows would have miched
off for the day, but Tommie *wanted* in, you see. He loved
his work!

Still, he knew what was expected of him, as an
Andrews, as a *Pirrie*.

[*Did he receive special treatment at Harland & Wolff's?*]

(*Sits forward*)
– Not at all, no special treatment! He was to make

6

it himself without favour or pull. But of course he was in the Connection and we had our eye on him. 'Punctuality,' I told him, 'is the politeness of Kings, the duty of gentlemen, the necessity of men of business.' My mother told me King Louis XIV said that. She wrote it down with all her other sayings and gave me the book. I'm never without it. (*Points to it on the table, lifts it, perhaps kisses it.*) I've been called a self-made man. No, my mother made me . . . Out there in the loneliness of Canada she lost my father but carried on and brought my sister and me back to Conlig and *raised us right*!

(*Sits back in reminiscence*) Tommie was loved in the Yard as well as in the family. *And* on the ships. The stewards presented him with a brand-new walking-stick they found him that obliging. They heard he was murdered with the varicose veins. He was his father's favourite. 'Well, big son, how are you?' my brother-in-law Tom would ask, proud as a peacock. Tommie wasn't noticeably big, oh, burly enough, active too, but he was big in heart. He had, to use an Ulster word you won't have heard, *naturality*. (*Ruminates*) I think those who loved his company had the opportunity to like *themselves.* He made those who loved him forget the back-streets they came from. They felt proud of him and proud of themselves. (*Sings – but falters at end of the couplet into speech. Actor can provide a suitable tune*) –

> 'Oh Tommie, Tommie Andrews we are all so proud of you,
> And to say we have the finest ship that e'er was built, is true' –

7

Dear old Doctor O'Loughlin from Dublin, a pal of
Tommie's, wrote that song with the Purser of the
Oceanic. (Sadly) The good doctor was lost too. *(Rallies.
Permits himself the suggestion of an awkward take-off of the
'honest Ulsterman' and a Belfast accent with the second syllable
of 'Belfast' accentuated, and a slightly condescending chuckle)*
(Rises)

   'A Queen's Island Trojan, he worked to the last;
   Very proud we all feel of him here in Belfast.'

(Head shaking) What was it made them write verses
about Tommie?
(Pause, soberly)
Yes, it was their pride in him. Tommie was spared the
anger that some men let in to keep their sorrow at bay.
He was a hero in death so there must be villains in life.
They thought like that and made Ismay the villain-in-
chief. And indeed *(confiding, perhaps for the first time)*,
Ismay ought to have stayed with Tommie and Captain
Smith to the last. *(Breaks off, suddenly needing to establish
his own agenda. Signals it by resuming his seat)*
   . . . Look here, young man, I'm happy to tell you
what I remember about Tommie, the marvellous boy.
But we at Harland & Wolff haven't talked about what
happened for obvious reasons. There was that priest chap
showing his photographs and giving lectures and no
doubt making some money into the bargain. But no, we
told him, you must desist, we don't wish the memory
of this calamity to be perpetuated. We have ships to
build! He's a chaplain in the War now, I hear, far better

employed. Doing something *for* morale, not sapping it. (*Anger plants itself*) Some Presbyterian minister in New York thought the steamship men like myself . . . listen (*Rises and rifles quickly through his journal and reads, with mounting indignation*) –

'. . . they could receive no severer punishment than to be compelled to read and re-read the harrowing details of the ship's last two hours.'

A Christian man! This minister *revelled* in his picture of the poor devils who drowned –

'their glassy glaring eyes staring at the furnishings of the sunken palace, priceless jewels become the playthings of the queer creatures that sport in the dark depths.'

Do we want to aid and abet this kind of thing? My mother's *people* were Presbyterians, her uncle a minister for heaven's sake, but the things they said . . . and just as bad in Belfast! One minister sneered that the ship (*voice rising*) had a riding school, a rose garden, a vinery! And all at the expense of lifeboats! Nonsense. Ismay tried to put them right on that. We had the regulation number of boats. Anyway, the Board of Trade had only to say the word. In Harland & Wolff we can build fourteen lifeboats of the largest size *simultaneously* in six weeks! It was a *myth* that sank as much as a real ship! Alma White, that American preacher woman, said the ship was Britain herself, showed how British manhood was degenerating, had no muscle. She doesn't say! Well, we're showing *her* at Passchendaele!

(Holds his indignation then converts it into something positive. Looking at the interviewer, departing from his mandate, and with more emotion, even passion. He raises his hand to forestall an incoming question)

– No, let me say this – we are *proud* of what we put inside our ships! We know our customers. Colonel Astor, Ben Guggenheim, Charlie Hays, Issy Straus and the others on the maiden voyage – they needed to feel at home, or in some first-class hotel to conduct business. John Jacob Astor *owned* top-hole hotels, for goodness' sake, Charlie Hays presided over the Grand Trunk Railway, and wanted to drive it all the way from the Atlantic to the Pacific – greatest railroad genius in Canada! John Thayer, of the Pennsylvania Railroad. George Widener ran streetcars in Philadelphia – all on the maiden voyage and all on the move. Already the train can get you from New York to Chicago in 18 hours! We're shrinking the world, young man!

I travel through England and the Continent, staying in the finest hotels to see if we can emulate them on board our ships. That was what brought me here to Witley Park in nineteen and nine after the strange death of Whitaker Wright – The splendid interior! The magnificent palm house, the oak-panelled corridors, the elegant grand staircase! Lady Pirrie is not in love with Witley, I have to admit. But I adore it! Lloyd George has been to visit us – and *(even during the war this is a kind of boast)* . . . even the wretched Kaiser himself! And look – this smoking room *(waving his arm airily to his interlocutor to indicate that is where they now are)* – *under* the water!

You've no doubt noticed, young man, how like Witley is to the photographs of *Olympic* and her sisters. But what are the lounges and suites of the finest hotels? Copies of our stately homes! (*Bragging*) That is what we try to do with our magnificent ships!

All these carpings from the pulpit – beside the point! They missed the connection! The ships, the railways, the motor cars, hotels – they all connect! The Americans know this better than ourselves, with their magnificent hotels at the ports and railheads. (*He's on fire again*) Why, it's all like the electrical installation on our ships, connecting and charging almost everything. A network . . . of power and impulse! The world is speeding up, young man . . . linking up . . . . (*With weaving gestures*) Our ships for the White Star run from New York to Liverpool, Liverpool to Australia, Boston to the Mediterranean, New Zealand to Liverpool – I tell you, we are weaving the Anglo-Saxon world together!

I told them in Portland, Maine, I told Charlie Hays – if the port is made ready and the harbour deep enough I will build you enough ships in Belfast to haul all the freight you want to!

(*Warming to the themes of magnitude and power*) And all the while our ships grow – two hundred and ninety feet long, *three* hundred and ninety feet long, four hundred and *fifty* feet – *900* feet give or take! We have to dredge to berth them – so we do! You, young man, might live to see a fifteen-hundred foot boat! *They* grow, and the Yard grows to keep up with them. Their womb and cradle! (*on fire again*) The energy of men and the power of machines! We have over two thousand motors running now in the shipyard. Eighty-thousand pounds of water are evaporated *every hour* to keep them going! Does our reach exceed our grasp? – No! We've dug and channelled, built and expanded – four hundred men in '62, twelve thousand in 19 and 10! I can't tell you how many today, for obvious reasons. We're in the middle of a war.

(*Barely pausing*) That April was indeed a cruel month. But it wasn't the end of the world. That very summer when I went aboard the *Fionia*, I saw we must have her extraordinary engine. It was the future, Diesel's engine – I could see that! (*Animated*) Before the year was out I got Harland & Wolff the rights to the engine for the whole of the British Empire. We didn't sink in nineteen and twelve, young man, we *swam*! Set that down, young man, set that down!

(*Breathes*) Someone has written that I've built more ships and bigger ships than anyone since the days of Noah! (*Chuckles*) True. And the men of money make it possible! Why delude ourselves? When I hear about the idle rich on board my ships my blood could boil. Yes, we carry clubmen, wastrels some of them. But the fellows I'm talking about make things happen. And they are always curious to know how things on board *work* and are put together! John Astor was himself an inventor. *And* he wrote a novel set in Mars or somewhere, too, I hear – full of astounding machines and engines of the future. Took a lifebelt apart on the ship to show his young bride what the thing was made of and how it did its job. And he was a hero, too. Stepped back from the lifeboat and lit a cigarette. 'Join you later, dear,' he said. Richest man on board (*shaking his head in admiring recollection*) . . .

And of *course* we carry the poor as well. We make the most comfortable quarters for them they've ever had! And where are we carrying them to? To the New World where things are on the move and men of vision look from coast to coast!

I tell you, the fellow from Belfast forgot his congregation that Sunday. He must have – he saw the ship as a heap of scrap metal two miles under the waves. I read in the papers what he told them about our ship: (*Returns to his journal – and reads, scathingly*)

> 'Forsooth! The very name of the ship breathed the spirit of human self-conceit, the pride that cometh before a fall. How devils must laugh and angels must weep at the bombastic impertinence.'

But I know his congregation was *proud* of what we made!

The sumptuousness, the luxury, call it what you will – we *made* it in Belfast. A hundred and eighty men working on the carved panelling alone! (*Savouring the word*) – Craftsmanship! (*Resumes his chair*) 'The perils of prosperity', one minister said that Sabbath day: yes, but (*witheringly*) are the perils of poverty to be preferred? 'The gospel of materialism' another said. It isn't the gospel of materialism we preach at Queen's Island, but the gospel of work! (*Puts journal down*)

– Tommie? Tommie lived and *breathed* the gospel of
work. He wasn't alone. I learned it on my mother's knee.
She learned it from her father-in-law whose motto was
'Deeds, not words'.

Captain Pirrie escaped from the French in Napoleon's
war – came to Ulster, married a Morison of Sandyland
and settled at Conlig. He masterminded Victoria
Channel that made big shipping possible. (*A muscular
memory*) He poured a bottle of whiskey on it to christen
it. The spoil made Dargan's island. They renamed it
'Queen's Island' for the visit of the Empress in 1849. Yes,
it became our family motto – 'Deeds not Words'.

Tommie hung in his closet a copy of a poem – Here -

'Let me but do my work from day to day,
In field or forest, at the desk or loom,
In roaring market-place or tranquil room'

There's poetry for you!
(*Rises*)
'What we think, or what we know, or what we believe,
is in the end of little consequence. The only thing of
consequence is what we do.' That was on Tommie's
Christmas cards – from the writer Ruskin.

'Work', said Ruskin 'must be honest, useful and
cheerful.' Honest – well, Tommie was very hard on
any idlers or bad timekeepers in the Yard, docked
their wages and no mistake. Useful? When the great
ships move down the slipway, everyone, from the

humblest message-boy to the head draughtsman, sees
his handiwork before his very eyes. I remember when
Tommie was an apprentice he told my sister that he
didn't know who he'd work for – Harland & Wolff, J.P.
Morgan, White Star, the Congested Districts Board out
in the west – it was all the same to him: he didn't care a
hang, as long as he got the experience.

That was it: work wasn't an ordeal, a chore, but a
pleasure, like sailing.

[*Or playing cricket?*]

– Yes, or like playing cricket – he loved the green. He
was always cheerful. I remember his wife Nellie made
up an advertisement as if for the papers – 'To Let – the
starboard side of a double bed. Only those of a restful
disposition need apply'! Home at nightfall and away at
dawn. But she was having a jest. Work was *him*. That's
why he liked Van Dyke's little poem in his closet –

'I am the one by whom
This work can best be done in the right way.'

What self-assurance! A virtuoso in the *doing* part of
life was Tommie. I *know*. I came up through the ranks
myself, I showed him how. (*swagger*) – I went into
Sir Edward's firm as an apprentice at fifteen; and by
heavens, at twenty-seven I was master of the concern.
Like Tommie, I know the Firm from mast-head to keel.

No doubt Tommie had to come by his assurance
the hard way. I'm sure he suffered the same indignities

all apprentices suffer in that school of hard knocks.
(*Mimicking a boy's innocently keen yet wary voice*)

   – 'Mr Tomelty from the boiler shop sent me for a long
weight.' (*Chuckles*) A long wait it was too.

   'Mr Carnaghan sent me for a bucket of steam'. Even
when you thought you might be codded, you didn't
dare take the chance.

   'Mr O'Neill wants to know if you've a spare bubble
for a spirit-level'.

   Maybe they were getting their own back for their
own tribulations years before. A rough enough
schooling was the Yard: foul mouths sometimes, and
thievery, and hard fellows from Ballymacarett or the
Falls lifting their hand to you if you let them. Platers,
riveters, caulkers – tough fellows. Yet Tommie was at
home there, and took the troublemakers on when need
be. Oh, he wasn't above taking off his coat and squaring
up.

   (*Sits*) No, young sir, no better experience than
apprenticeship. Tommie was, like myself, by turns
(*telling them off on his fingers*) a joiner, a painter, a fitter,
a patternmaker, a blacksmith, a draughtsman. (*This to
be savoured -*) *Then* he bloomed amidst the clamour and
clatter, the motion and motley of the machine shops,
the hive of activity from morning til night. (*A sudden
memory*) 'The hive of activity'. (*Chuckles*) . . .

   – Tommie kept bees as a boy in the sheltered garden
of Ardara – nine hives he had for his honey bees. He
was as wholehearted about that as about everything
else – threw himself into it. Had to read the best books
on the subject, he read (*in mock awe*) *The Life of the Bee*

by Monsieur Maeterlinck. I was so amused I borrowed his copy. I recall the bees teaching the writer 'the indefatigable organisation of life, the lesson of ardent and disinterested work'.

Now, an apprentice might think he's on the moulding-loft floor, being patterned and cut to somebody else's specifications. Not so, you're making *yourself*. When you've completed your apprenticeship you're a self-made man. Tommie was a self-made man.

But then, Belfast is a self-made *city*, and grows out of its clothes almost as soon as it puts them on. Belfast has beaten the proudest cities of the Empire with no God-given advantages – no raw materials or resources. And no doles from the treasury to help her either – no, by her own energy, raising *herself* up to industrial eminence! Belfast produces the ships, the machines, the machines that *make* machines, *out of itself*, as . . . bees . . . produce . . . honey.

We invited the countryside to work in Ballymacarrett. Then we beckoned the *world* to us – Edward Harland came from Newcastle upon Tyne, Gustav Wolff came from Hamburg, Chevalier Heyn from Danzig.

The principals of the Firm took to Belfast like ducks to water. Or should I say, like Harland & Wolff ships to the sea. Gustav perhaps took to it excessively (*affecting a German accent*)

'You may talk off your Edinburg and zee beauties of
  Perth,
And all zee large cities famed on zee earth,

17

But gif me my house, though it be in a garret,
In zee pleasant surroundings of Ballymacarrett.'

Gustav foisted that on us when Belfast made him an honorary burgess.

[*Mr Andrews never became a principal of Harland & Wolff?*]

(*Pause. Pirrie is rather ambushed by this question that punctures his self-satisfaction. Turns and resumes his seat*) – No, you're quite right, I didn't make Tommie a principal in the Firm. I chose John Kempster instead. (*Slightly ruffled; rises; perhaps to stall his answer, goes upstage with cigar to get a drink, helps himself, turns to answer*) I thought Tommie was not quite ready. (*Brandishing the empty snifter*) A sterling designer and engineer, top of the heap, but perhaps not quite *worldly* enough. Kempster is an engineer who knows his economics. And the Yard, remember, is business, *big* business.
(*Pours drink*)
Don't listen to anyone who says I passed Tommie and Carlisle over because I was a Home Ruler and they were Unionists! I tried to keep all that away from shipbuilding. *Yes*, I joined the Liberal Party but I assure you I was for the Union. Why, I was *nominated* as a unionist in nineteen and two in South Belfast! (*emphatic*) I tell you, our shipyard *is* the Union! (*Diversionary tactic*)
   – When we don't make our own machines we draw on the manufacturing genius of England and Scotland – (*reciting the harsh native British names as if poetry*) –

Wadsworth of Bolton,
Scriven of Leeds,
Arrol of Glasgow,
Wadkin of Nottingham,
Craven of Manchester . . .

And why should a man be only one thing but not
the other? (*hotly defensive*) Yes, I *did* come out for Home
Rule. I don't deny it. Sir Arthur Conan Doyle and I
signed that statement for the press after the sinking when
the Home Rule Bill was going through – we said that
Home Rule would *complete* the Empire not destroy it!

(*The salesman, rallying*) I was convinced, and *am*
convinced, that we can preach the gospel of work and
the benefits of iron and steel, even to the farmers, to *all*
the island. When I was Lord Mayor of Belfast I wanted
no one excluded – '*Let* Catholics into the City Council',
I said. What I wanted was my city, and Ulster, to be,
well, a *Firm*, or a very engine, oiled and smoothly
working. When I said, and did so no doubt too many
times, 'Go in and win!' I said that to *all* the youth of the
country.

When I saw unionists crouching behind Carson for
shelter, I invited Churchill and Redmond to Belfast.
Unionist ruffians pelted me in the streets with eggs and
Ardglass herrings . . . Called me a traitor. 'Lord Lundy!'
Those were difficult days . . .
(*Lapses into a slightly ruffled silence, and puffs at his cigar,
forgetting it unlit. A little stage business while his mood softens.
Then after a few moments resumes, in a different key*)
'No, Tommie was a leader, but not political. Tommie
simply rose to the occasion. Any occasion. I remember

H. G. Wells said a new kind of soldier will lead our society, a sober engineering man. Well, Tommie already *was* that kind of soldier. I see him in my mind's eye. Overseeing everything at horn-blow, with his bowler hat on his head spattered with paint, a roll of ship's plans under his arm. I saw him once at a gangplank with three or four thousand workers swarming across it like bees, and a guard rope gave way over a ninety-foot drop, and Tommie's tremendous voice rose above the noise: 'Halt! Stand back!' and he held the plank clear until the rope was replaced, like some Horatio of the Yard.

Shipping business, you see . . . management of men. Yet he thought of the men as pals. I fostered the friendship of the men myself: thought it useful should there be friction or strikes. He followed my example. But Tommie went farther and seemed reluctant to appear *different* from them. I must say, I've had no such reluctance as time goes on. At all costs we have ships to build. It needs tremendous discipline . . . and authority . . . – and *efficiency.*

(*Resumes his seat. Has a sudden enthusiastic memory*) Oh yes, *efficiency!* I remember the vampire man came and saw us and was very impressed. The scale of operations stunned him. He came when the *Adriatic* was almost finished and we had all of nine ships on the stocks, so that would have been . . . oh, nineteen and seven. Tommie was one of our men who showed him around. If I'd known he was a famous author I'd have had the pleasure myself. Yes, he was impressed, especially by the boiler shops – well, his name was Stoker, after all, so I'm not surprised.

But what took him to the fair was the fact that we paid 12,000 workers every Friday afternoon *in ten minutes!* Bram Stoker thought we had organised everything so well that we made the mere building of the *ships* child's play. Something *to* that. *Interdependence* was the key, he saw − great, various, interdependent *work*: he revelled when he saw it in Belfast!

I recently got around to reading his famous novel. And there it all is! For how is Dracula beaten? By efficiency! By the use of proven business firms, by the advances in applied science − the cable, the Underground, the portable typewriter, the Winchester repeating rifle, the phonograph . . . Those who hunt Dracula are a *Firm*, indeed very nearly a *family* Firm, and they triumph in the end. Dracula is of the old superstitious past, managing director of a top-down bloodless workforce, and the Firm run him to earth at last, the job done. Out of business after a thousand years. (*Delighted . . . fist into palm, the deal done*)

(*Rises, goes to sideboard or bookshelf, collects magazine, turns, tapping its cover and announcing its title:* <u>The World's Work</u>.)

Stoker was mesmerised by our timber store (*Rifles to the correct page of his journal*) −

'Here may be seen fine-grained yellow pine from Canadian slow-growing forests, great teak balks from Rangoon; enormous trunks, roughly squared by the axe, of giant mahogany from Honduras; hardwoods of beautiful texture and pattern from Californian mountain woods, from Pacific Islands, from tropical rivers. The colour of the dry dust of

yellow pine and the damp dust of teak blend and give a
strange and unique aroma to the place'.

(*Pirrie savours this. Then makes his biggest point with relish
and pride*) –

Ah, the scenes and scents of the big world!

We bring the world to Belfast and send it back out
again – ship-shaped and to *our* specifications – moulded
and made, caulked and riveted, scarphed and fettled
– its parts configured and made into one – sailing or
steaming out, as perfect as we can make it.

And as beautiful! Wattie Wilson, one of our original
partners, used to say that our ships should be like the
salmon – the aristocrats of the fish kingdom. And
Wattie should know – retired to grow orchids, he did,
marvelling at their lovely shapes.
(*Sits*) . . . .

Yeats! Yeats and those other fellows in Dublin turn
their noses up at what we do, and think us merely
spreaders of materialism, our lives all mixed grills and
double whiskies. (*Has an ironic sip from his brandy snifter.*)
But I'll put our *ship*wrights up against their *play*wrights
any time. As for poetry – we find *our* poetry in the roar
of the iron forge and the clang of the Nasmyth hammer.
If they want our ships, why they can help us build 'em!
Carlisle and I went to Dublin several times to see if we
could set up shop there. Tommie would have been a
splendid man in Dublin.

I think the fine fellows over in Dublin are taking the
country the wrong way, turning their backs on industry
and hard work. *I say*, 'go into the South and win and

take our industry to share with them!'

That fellow Erskine Childers, who knows his boats, has turned republican now and cocks a snook at the Empire. But I know he came to Queen's Island and saw my nephew Tommie at close quarters, saw his mastery of the detail and the ensemble, and was very impressed by him. Well, the Firm too is an 'ensemble' (*mock-savouring the foreign-sounding word*). We call this now 'the division of labour' and every firm should practise it. Gustav made his little joke about it once upon a time at a launching (*Again, the German-Belfast accent*)

'Mr Chairman, Sir Edvard Harland builds zee ships for our firm; Mr Pirrie makes zee speeches, and as for me (*Pirrie waves his cigar*), Ja, I smoke zee cigars for the firm.'

(*Laughs*) A witty fellow – for a German.

It helps it think that so many of us at the top are kith and kin – the Harlands, the Carlisles, the Pirries, the Andrews – (*gesturing by meshing his hands*) we mesh, you might say, like the compound engine. Occasionally the parts need oil! – but mostly we run smooth. And whole families work below us in the Yard. Sons follow fathers, brothers follow brothers, so that each man has a compound interest in our success, you might say.

[*Is this entirely fair, hiring relatives?*]

– No, no, this is not cheating or nepotism – every cousin or son or brother-in-law in the Connection has

to prove his worth. It's true of all the factories in Belfast.
Is there a better system of manufacture? If so, I don't
know of it. It helps keep the socialists at bay. (*Waving his
cigar*) Perhaps it has even kept our savage politics at bay.
We came through the riots of '64 and '72, of '93 *and* 19
and 12. It's hard for anyone in Ireland to get a clear run
at a revolution. The whole place is a family Firm. While
we stay productive and hardworking we'll pull through.
We did then and we will now, in this terrible war.

The days of pull and influence I hope are gone. You
rise through the ranks by merit. Tommie himself knew
that. Self-help, that's the ticket.

Every man his chance! The boy from Conlig and the
wilds of Canada has had his fair share of honours and
rewards. I think of it as being top of the class. I don't say
we *finish* equal, but if we *start* equal, isn't that enough?
We go *in* and win if we can. And if we help others
along the way? Freddy Blackwood – (*to the interviewer*)
the Marquis of Dufferin – back in Clandeboye after
his great days in the Empire, called for a new hospital
for Belfast in 1896. Lady Pirrie plunged in to raise the
money. Seven years later the Royal Victoria Hospital
was opened by the late King. You *could say* that Harland
& Wolff built that great institution.

Poor Dufferin died the year before the hospital
opened its doors. Swindled out of thousands by
Whitaker Wright who built the house we're sitting in.

[*Who was Whitaker Wright?*]

– Wright? Wright had a humble start, by thirty-one

24

was a millionaire. Rode high after making his money in Colorado silver. Back in England he floated one company after another and set himself up next door to my friend Lord Londond'ry in Park Lane. He wanted to move in the best circles. (*A pause, perhaps because this is a little close to home*) Built this extraordinary house – (*gesturing around the room*)

(*Rises*) Then his luck changed. Tried to speculate his way out. All quite unethical. He crashed and sank and took the good Marquess and others with him. Hid in his own ice-house. (*Pointing to signify its closeness*) Fled to New York. Brought back and was sentenced to seven years. But he defrauded even justice. He swallowed a capsule of cyanide in the courtroom!

Money and standing without conscience, without courage. (*A little too emphatic, perhaps to cover his own eager rise up the social ranks. Then a creative pause to return to base*)

Well, Tommie didn't flee or hide. He was in plain view after the ship crashed, doing all he could, ever practical. Trying to keep everything shipshape to the end.

(*Vigorous re-enactment*) –

'We've only a couple of hours', he told Captain Smith, 'clear the boats'.

'See that the passengers put on warm clothing and have their life-belt – and get them to the boat-deck', he told a stewardess.

'Women and children first', he told the men at boat after boat.

'Get into the boats, ladies'

'Get into the boat', he told the stewardess Miss Sloan

from Belfast and she did, fifteen minutes before the ship sank. Perhaps he remembered the freezing day at Ardara when he spent hours bringing his bees to safety from the hive to the house, capful after capful of them. I spoke to Miss Sloan afterwards and she told me that from the lifeboat the ship was like a swarming bee-hive, but the bees were men . . .

(*He warms to the narrative, accelerates, feeling entering in. The actor should convey a mounting surprise on Pirrie's part: these are new thoughts and feelings.*) Someone saw him on the way to the bridge to be with Captain Smith. He seems to have been everywhere. A steward saw him in the first-class smoking room, gazing at Wilkinson's magnificent painting of *Plymouth Harbour*, and spoke to him, but Tommie didn't answer. He was in another world. (*Pirrie is in another world now, too. He speaks in an odd preoccupied monologue.*) He had done all in this life he could do. It was horn-blow but he was on a ship without a gantry and a gangway home. I wasn't there. Nor Carlisle. Ismay had abandoned ship. How *alone* Tommie must have felt.

He was no fatalist so I'm sure he didn't accept what was about to happen in that sense. He thought we're free to make of ourselves what we can. And that of course required work, and the duty work demands – the most direct line to heaven. Nor did Tommie believe in original sin, this I know. There was no darkness behind us and no darkness in front of us. I just hope he felt no shame about the ship. No need to.

I believe Tommy, in front of that gallant painting, was standing to attention when the ship sank. A true soldier.

I told my sister — a finer fellow than Tommie never
lived. She and Tommie's father were sent hundreds of
letters of sympathy. One uncle wrote: 'There is not a
better boy in heaven'. A truer word was never spoken.
And now — (*coming to as it were*) why, it's all of five years!
— he's coming to the end of a different apprenticeship
and no doubt getting ready to make heaven shipshape.
(*Long pause; what follows is heartfelt*)
I thank you for coming here, young man. We don't
want the memory of that calamity to be . . . . But we
should keep dear Tommie's memory fresh. My mother
wrote for me (*points to the small notebook*): 'God gives us
memory that we might have roses in December'. And
memories of Tommie are roses indeed . . . But I will
own up to nightmares since the ship . . . (*Halting, then
unburdening, slowly and painfully*) Unbearable to me is the
thought of our boy Tommie still on that ship, borne
under the waves, departing on that interminable voyage
into the abyss . . . (*Lengthy pause, — recovering, speaking the
verse slowly and deliberately, as epitaph*)

    'All the hives deserted, all the music fled . . .
    This is life, belovéd: first a sheltered garden,
        Then a troubled journey,
    Joy and pain of seeking, and at last we sleep' . . .

Lights down

Afterword

It is always difficult to clarify the particular opacities of a given society or culture. It can be even harder to describe the stratagems by which that culture seeks to explain itself to itself – a task which, in Northern Ireland, has become a matter as much of public policy (as a means of mitigating senses of historical disadvantage and managing the memory of recent and not-so-recent civic violence) as it is a matter for historians and writers.

It is simply not possible to understand the roots of recent decades of conflict in Northern Ireland and their associated impacts in Ireland and in Great Britain, without spending time with the very intense and intimate proximity of key world events to the tiny streets and busy population of a small classic 19th century city and its modest environs. To say this is not to privilege a certain 'take' on history, or claim a special status for a particular engagement in some of the global dramas of the 20th Century

It may come as a surprise to note that, as the rest of the world geared up for sombre and reflective national moments connected with the centenaries of the First World War, with an obvious commencement date of August 2014, Northern Ireland had already been engaged for some years in what government and civic authorities and agencies had styled the 'decade of centenaries'.

This concept was derived as a response to the keen

awareness, taught by experience, that particular years in Irish and British history harboured significant cargoes of inflammatory material for current generations; that the act of memory was no neutral engagement with an agreed narrative, whatever about the historians' primacy of 'facts'. Dates such as, for example, 1690 (the Battle of the Boyne), 1798 (a major rebellion in Ireland against British government), 1916 (the Easter Rising in Dublin, the foundation event of the modern state of Ireland), all had and have their own very contemporary resonances and nuances, all of them contested, all of them potential opportunities for reflection or conflict or both.

Aware of these matters and protective of the recently-established power-sharing mechanism constructed by the Good Friday or Belfast Agreement in 1998, but given renewed impetus by an Executive established in 2007, both governmental and civic bodies recognised that a strategic framework for managing how these events might be recognised, would be both prudent and potentially fruitful in the face of a sequence of looming difficult centenaries.

The 'decade' really began in 2009 with reflections on a distant but no less intimate historical event – the Plantation of Ulster in 1609. That event and its relative low-key and successful outworking saw the sequence quickly fill out with potential content – '2012 The Ulster Covenant', '2014 The Outbreak of War', '2016 The Easter Rising and the Battle of the Somme', '2017 Messines'.

The decade was assisted greatly, it must be said, by the historic 2011 State Visit by HM The Queen to Ireland, during which she paid public tribute to the dead of the

Easter Rising at the Garden of Remembrance in Dublin – an occurrence of extraordinary symbolic and emotional power. It also set a tone and a template for how subsequent commemorations might be effectively handled and designed a set of permissions that might allow communities uncomfortable with the risk-taking that memory entails to step over the line.

Though 2016 contained what many felt would be the most testing double-centenary, that now seems to have been overly pessimistic. With vast resources, both the UK-wide Somme commemorations and the Irish Government's detailed, sensitive and vigorously inclusive re-memorisation of 1916, assisted the year to pass, as the news bulletins increasingly say in Northern Ireland, 'without incident'.

The list of centenaries rolls out predictably once the core idea is clear. Add in suffrage, the influenza epidemic of 1918, armistice, the partition of Ireland, and the list quickly proliferates. But what was less predictable as a contested commemoration was one other centenary which took place in 2012, one which wouldn't appear to bear any of the toxic freight other centenaries might be expected to carry.

But it is for this very reason that it is central to understanding the roots of conflict to be aware of the vast psychic presence of the liner RMS *Titanic* in the culture of Northern Ireland.

I am not going to labour metaphors of icebergs and sunken memory or diving missions or search-and-recovery exercises; or even to dwell on the peculiar hold sea wrecks maintain on the imaginations of Ulster people, whether it be the Spanish Armada galleon *Girona*, under water off Lacada Point, near the Giant's Causeway, discovered 50 years ago this year; the MV *Princess Victoria* which went down in 1953 in the Irish Sea with 133 lives lost, subject of an elegy by the poet Roy McFadden; the role the 'big ship' plays in the poetry of contemporary Belfast poet and T. S. Eliot Prize-winner Sinéad Morrissey ('the sheer cliff-/face of the ship still enveloped in its scaffolding/backside against the launching cradle'); but it is important to say that one of the most important contemporary interpreters of the mythology of the 'big ship' is John Wilson Foster himself, whose *Titanic: Culture and Calamity* (2016) and *The Age of Titanic: Cross-Currents in Anglo-American Culture* (2002) are just two of this thinker's extended meditations on the perennial grip the ship sustains on the popular and aesthetic imagination. As one critic put it, Foster generated 'a brilliant extensive study of the cultural vortex which surrounded, and surrounds to this day, the making of the *Titanic* and its terrible fate'.

As an organisation described as a 'non-departmental public body', at 'arm's length' from government, the Arts Council was awake to the potential for organisations funded by it to play their part in the process of commemoration; but, of course, would never be in the position of initiating proposals itself, let alone delivering directly on any artistic response. The colossal brand-new Titanic Belfast interpretative centre was planned to open a few weeks prior to the actual date of the ship's sinking, and the city had devised a programme of *Titanic*-related festivities which gave another context to any conventional rememberings of the tragedy itself.

Among the events were a spectacular lightshow at the very dock the ship had been built; *Titans*, a new play by Jimmy McAleavey; a reading by the German poet Hans Magnus Enzensberger of his epic poem *Der Untergang der Titanic* perilously on a barge on the River Lagan at the docks; Rosemary Jenkinson's *White Star*, which played the Lyric Theatre Belfast; the première of composer Philip Hammond's intense and wistful *Requiem for the Lost Souls of the* Titanic; Dan Gordon's *The Boat Factory*; Owen McCafferty's verbatim play *Titanic* (*Scenes from the British Wreck Commissioner's Enquiry, 1912*); and *Land of Giants*, an epic multi-media extravaganza which played out to an audience of 18,000 at the Titanic slipway in June.

With the opening also of The MAC, the state-of-the-art 'metropolitan' arts centre in the city's burgeoning cultural quarter later in the year, 2012 was seen not only as a moment of global attention on the city, thanks to the obvious Hollywood melodrama and genuinely melancholic pilgrimage of the big ship, but also as an opportunity for civic re-vision, community remembering and, importantly, 'national' re-branding.

This was the context in which it first became known that the academic, literary critic, 'cultural commentator' and 'public intellectual' John Wilson Foster, was at work on a drama.

His own presence as a major influence in the historical evaluation of core literary texts in the Ulster and Irish canon was already a formidable and enriching one. *Forces and Themes in Ulster Fiction* (1974) and *Fictions of the Irish Literary Revival* (1987) have proven indispensable companions to an extensive range of imaginative documents which have helped shape ideas of identity, allegiance and belonging among subsequent generations of writers and, by extension, an attentive public; they have, in fact, joined them in performing something of that function themselves.

But playwriting is another thing entirely. In addition to the challenge – and the risk – of the very act of crafting a play, there was what seemed the rather unappetising theme. A thinker so well versed in the mythology of the *Titanic* itself could have been forgiven giving in to the temptation of joining the ranks of writers compelled to find some new dimension of irony or suffering in what is the capacious resource of the ship's journey itself. But Foster chose a particular evening in the life of, certainly one of the central figures in Belfast's industrial history, but hardly – it seemed – one of the pivotal figures in the direction of the culture as a whole; and, it seemed equally clear, not a life bothered particularly with its own dramatic peaks and troughs.

Could anything, in fact, be less intriguing than the musings of a stuffy Edwardian businessman who was, in reality, the very epitome of a Victorian self-made tycoon, overwrought with religion and pomposity and whose reputation down the century after his death has been coloured irrevocably by his nonchalant dismissal of queries about the appropriate number of lifeboats on the ill-fated vessel his firm had built?

As it turned out, not only did Foster manage to enter the remote temporal and psychological universe at the centre of which was William Pirrie as a complex and haunted individual, but he brought to the narrative the very real instincts of a storyteller and, in the midst of stern examinations of Ulster – and Canadian – attitudes and mores, brought an overwhelming compassion to an interior life most stereotypes would have denied existed. The magnate's reflections on the death of the great ship and of his beloved nephew, Thomas Andrews, the vessel's designer who chose to go down with it, are by turns infuriating, admirable, dismaying, gripping and memorable.

The original production of *A Better Boy*, commissioned by Belfast Titanic Company, produced by Kabosh and starring Lalor Roddy, played for a week at the peak of the Titanic Belfast Festival, from 9th–15th April 2012. It was a theatrical success, described as 'beautifully written, frank, uncompromising and fascinating in its personal insights and reminiscences', Pirrie's monologue seen 'as much a eulogy to industry as . . . to his nephew.'

Happily, the potential of the play to exceed its 'occasional' character as a moment in the great narrative of *Titanic*'s recovery by the City of Belfast, was quickly perceived – and not only by the playwright. The Arts Council's attention was drawn to the value of the work as a possible showcase for indigenous talent under the auspices of the Office of the Northern Ireland Bureau in Brussels – the headquarters of Northern Ireland's First Minister and Deputy First Minister in the capital of the European Union and the prime site for the promotion of the cultural imagination on a platform much larger than anything that could be offered within Northern Ireland itself.

The play text was revisited by the playwright in the light of its actual performance before audiences; a new production company was sourced; and the whole venture received a huge boost with the involvement of one of the most distinguished actors of stage and screen, Ian McElhinney, in the daunting role of William Pirrie.

The new version of the play was tested in the Brian Friel Theatre at Queen's University in the first week of December 2013 and played to full houses in the acclaimed Bozar Theatre in Brussels on 16th and 17th December.

It was clear that the revisited version of the script had benefited greatly from the playwright's reflection even on what had been very satisfying outings the previous year in Belfast.

It remains an hour or so, in performance, of wonderful company. So much is conveyed so quickly, so naturally, so economically, with so many modulations, all strangely befitting the restraint and reserve and poise of Pirrie himself, who emerges briskly and memorably out of a narrative almost wholly focused elsewhere – on 'Tommie', industry, politics, wealth, work and war. The imposing figure of Pirrie, albeit self-inflated to a degree, paradoxically only increases in volume as the play develops, emerging out of the fog of time and myth and stereotype as an even more memorable – and human – character.

What occurs in the play is a unique moment. The history of Ulster in particular is replete with 'figures of stature' – industrialists, pioneers, inventors, divines, scientists, explorers, soldiers . . . a succession of individuals, in a few cases heroic, in many cases indispensable, in some cases venal, in all cases flawed. Also, it must be admitted, what history has handed down to us in its conventional manner is almost exclusively masculine; and this has had the effect of characterising or, indeed, caricaturing, the 'Ulster' temper itself as brusque and stocky, and its possessor perhaps even as a bullying patriarch, with no time for frills or fripperies; certainly not a Gaelic speaker, for example; certainly not a rebel; certainly not a woman.

Murland, Ferguson, Mulholland, Kelvin, Herdman, Crozier, Dunlop, Johnston, Richardson, Barbour, Workman, Dunbar, Boyd, Harland, Cooke, Mackie, McCrum . . . This is a roster of formidable and, in many ways, opaque individuals. Their sombre and impressive homes have disappeared; their businesses are swallowed up in other less bold ventures or rendered completely obsolete by later innovations; their names survive only on the odd monument or garish window in a church no longer in use. Foster and Pirrie are acutely aware of the potency of these names:

> When we don't make our own machines we draw
> on the manufacturing genius of England and
> Scotland — (*reciting the harsh native British names as if*
> *poetry*) —
>> Wadsworth of Bolton,
>> Scriven of Leeds,
>> Arrol of Glasgow,
>> Wadkin of Nottingham,
>> Craven of Manchester . . .

Pirrie of Belfast himself is of their number. While flamboyant historical figures such as Henry Joy McCracken, Hugh O'Neill and Wolfe Tone have found contemporary voices in Irish theatre through the likes of Stewart Parker and Brian Friel, the 'Ulster Protestant' as Protestant has struggled to find a medium adequate to the various stories of diligent hard work, financial speculation, chance, respectability and sound economics, which might allow that version of historical experience, that trajectory of 'national' development – outside the melodrama of social or political violence – to find contemporary expression.

Fair enough, they may not be the most engaging mechanisms for human empathy. But recent surprising successes scored by St John Ervine (1883-1971) with his plays *Mixed Marriage* (1911) at the Lyric in Belfast and the Finborough in London (a four-week sell-out run in October 2011) and *John Ferguson* (1915) also at the Finborough in 2014, show that period pieces at least can shed their mannerisms sufficiently to engage new and unfamiliar audiences in rediscovering not only the works themselves but also the strange peoples these plays illuminate.

Coupled with that new attraction for the tale of the mogul, Foster's *A Better Boy*, similarly, engages a different cadence of dramatic encounter. Pirrie's internal reflection under the interrogation, as it were, of a sensation-seeking reporter, exposes, in Foster's structuring, a man at once supremely self-confident and utterly riven by a doubt verging on despair. For whole moments, the rhetorical grandeur of Pirrie's utterance brings the audience, in a quite exhilarating way, to a vivid sense of the epic values – moral, political, social, cultural, religious – which drove individuals such as he to such feats of empire-building. For a moment, in fact, Pirrie's urgency and zeal come down clearly through the century which now, finally, separates us from the actual date of this encounter.

For a moment, we live wholly in his world. But only for a moment. The rationale of this most rational man for why things happen in the world collapses under the very pointed emptiness of his own achievement.

Except it is no mean achievement. One of the pleasures of the play is the opportunity to coincide with one of the great visionaries of the last century, even though, for us, it is a 'steampunk' vision. In our day, where there are exciting and massively-popular revivals of Victorian or Napoleonic classics – *Sherlock* (2010-), *Doctor Thorne* (2016-), *Poldark* (2015-), for example – and strange hybrids such as *Ripper Street* (2012-16), *Whitechapel* (2009-13), *Mr Selfridge* (2013-) and *Downton Abbey* (2010-15) – it is appropriate to encounter no less a Victorian 'imagineer' than Bram Stoker ('the vampire man') in Foster's world and to find his arrival explicitly addressed by the great Pirrie in a nimble and clever account of how even the supernatural is overcome by technology:

> For how is Dracula beaten? By efficiency! By the use of proven business firms, by the advances in applied science – the cable, the Underground, the portable typewriter, the Winchester repeating rifle, the phonograph . . . Those who hunt Dracula are a Firm, indeed very nearly a family Firm, and they triumph in the end. Dracula is of the old superstitious past, managing director of a top-down bloodless workforce, and the Firm run him to earth at last, the job done. Out of business after a thousand years. (*Delighted . . . fist into palm, the deal done*)

The great ship itself is a ghost in the text, to be navigated around, but the power it represents draws Pirrie ever back into its metal embrace, just as it dragged other great figures of the age, his contemporaries and friends, down with it to the bottom of the sea:

> John Astor was himself an inventor. And he wrote
> a novel set in Mars or somewhere, too, I hear – full
> of astounding machines and engines of the future.
> Took a lifebelt apart on the ship to show his young
> bride what the thing was made of and how it did
> its job. And he was a hero, too. Stepped back from
> the lifeboat and lit a cigarette. 'Join you later, dear,'
> he said. Richest man on board (*shaking his head in
> admiring recollection*).

The great ship was built in a shipyard intimately identified down the 20th century with Ulster Protestant industry and the grand values of the Empire and with increasingly less savoury associations as the new state of Northern Ireland emerged out of savage communal violence in the 1920s as an embattled jurisdiction. That state then settled in to almost 50 years of increasingly nervous and contested democracy, culminating in the upheavals in the late 1960s, followed by almost 40 years of a stand-off on the verge of civil war; of bombings, shooting attacks, paramilitary engagements, armed police, regular soldiers, body searches, hunger strikes, atrocities, and, eventually, a protracted 'peace process' the outworkings of which are still maturing.

The wreck itself had only been located in 1985. Its

reappearance then as a physical artefact of huge proportions to match its mythic scale and the return of the *Titanic* story to the attention of 'global storytelling' in 1997 with James Cameron's CGI masterpiece raised questions of 'ownership', less of the remains or its relics, than of the myth.

The city of Belfast was reluctant to associate itself at first with what was strangely characterised, even though it was a source of pride for many in the shipyard's heritage, as 'a failure'. There was reluctance among the nationalist Catholic community to embrace a story which might glorify the technological innovations of people who were Protestant, culturally and politically dominant, and an industry in which they felt, with reason, they had been allowed to play only a tangential role. Celebrating the *Titanic* would, it was felt, be tantamount to celebrating the very existence of Northern Ireland and what it represented.

As it happened, the positive legacy of the ship and the shipyards was moved to the centre, as political forces across the divide recognised the value of the *Titanic* brand and its many associations worldwide as a potential attraction for a city which was surviving its reputation as a dangerous centre of conflict. The local riposte to the charge that the ship was flawed from the outset remains a charming and humorous rejoinder to the darker aspects of its history: 'It was alright when it left here.'

As you would expect, Foster's text is alert to all the inflections of this political, cultural and social heritage; but with a refreshing subtlety and some wry ironies. Home Rule was a version of limited independence which stopped well short of independent statehood for Ireland; but support for it was enough to raise serious objections. Few would expect to find that Pirrie – on the cusp of elevation to the peerage – was himself in some eyes already 'disloyal' because he was an avowed Home Ruler in a city and among a class and a population almost violently Unionist. Pirrie was wealthy enough and powerful enough to espouse what he saw as an unavoidable economic and political strategy:

> Don't listen to anyone who says I passed Tommie and Carlisle over because I was a Home Ruler and they were Unionists! I tried to keep all that away from shipbuilding. Yes, I joined the Liberal Party but I assure you I was for the Union. Why, I was nominated as a unionist in nineteen and two in South Belfast! (*emphatic*) I tell you, our shipyard *is* the Union! (*Diversionary tactic*)
>
>   . . . Yes, I did come out for Home Rule. I don't deny it. Sir Arthur Conan Doyle and I signed that statement for the press after the sinking when the Home Rule Bill was going through – we said that Home Rule would complete the Empire not destroy it!

But politicking and posturing on the 'big talk' of the day is always trumped by the 'small talk' of private life and one leaves *A Better Boy* with an almost overwhelming sadness. Not even the ingenuity of the great figures of his day could forestall the vast wreckage of World War One which haunts the text any more than all the resources of Pirrie's own company could prevent the catastrophe of 15th April 1912 and the deaths of those 1,517 people, among whom was the great entrepreneur's own nephew, Tommie.

If there is one abiding image in the play which succinctly captures the tiny futility of human agency in circumstance of accident, it is the recurring trope of bees, which Tommie 'kept . . . as a boy in the sheltered garden of Ardara – nine hives he had for his honey bees'. The narrative builds at that point in the text to a wonderful pathos, as Pirrie recounts Andrews's final visible moments on board:

> 'Get into the boat,' he told the stewardess Miss Sloan from Belfast and she did, fifteen minutes before the ship sank. Perhaps he remembered the freezing day at Ardara when he spent hours bringing his bees to safety from the hive to the house, capful after capful of them. I spoke to Miss Sloan afterwards and she told me that from the lifeboat the ship was like a swarming bee-hive, but the bees were men.

One of the subtle skills of a playwright is to let the actor find the emotion loaded in the lines; in other words, not to place too much stress on what should arrive in performance as a sudden thought, utterly unanticipated, utterly new. It is a mark of Foster's ability that he recognised the potential of that image, managed it and then – with restraint and caution – allowed the lines themselves to do their talking on both his and Pirrie's behalf.

All this is a far cry from the often sullen meditations

academic study or studies prompt! This work is a real play, a drama, and it is all the more forceful by being marked by subtlety and restraint and understatement and genuine empathy both for lost generations and an age.

A Better Boy remains an important thing for our culture in Northern Ireland, Ireland and Great Britain and it is an entertaining, challenging, companionable, surprising and elegant thing. It is a delight now that its text is available for scrutiny and the potential of future production.

Damian Smyth
Head of Literature & Drama
Arts Council of Northern Ireland

William J. (Lord) Pirrie

W. J. Pirrie was born in Quebec City, Canada in 1847 to
Eliza Montgomery of County Antrim and James Pirrie of
County Down but was returned to northern Ireland by
his widowed mother on the death of her husband.

By his own wish, he left school in Belfast at fifteen
and was apprenticed to the young shipbuilding firm of
Harland & Wolff. By the age of twenty-two he was head
draughtsman and a firm's partner at twenty-seven; in his
late forties he became chairman of the then large and
famous yard and was recognised as the foremost British
shipbuilder. His business genius also came to be recognised: it was Pirrie who in 1902 in cooperation with
J. Pierpont Morgan masterminded the Syndicate, a con-
sortium of shipping companies known as International
Mercantile Marine and which included the White Star
Line for which Harland & Wolff built its ever-larger and
faster liners, culminating in *Olympic* and *Titanic*.

Shipbuilding did not entirely satisfy his passion for
making, and he supervised the design and building of the
famous Royal Victoria Hospital and was a motive force
behind the creation of the majestic Belfast City Hall. Un-
fulfilled in business even by immensely successful ventures, Pirrie like many leading Ulster businessmen of the
day engaged with politics and public life: by 1917 (and
before he suffered financial setbacks and left organisa-
tional disarray with his death, fittingly at sea - off Cuba

in 1924) he had been honorary treasurer of the Ulster Defence Union, Harbour Commissioner, Lord Mayor of Belfast, High Sherriff for the County of Antrim and then of County Down, His Majesty's Lieutenant for the City of Belfast, President of the Chamber of Shipping of the United Kingdom, Comptroller of the Household at Dublin Castle, Pro-Chancellor of The Queen's University of Belfast. Harland & Wolff flourished during the Great War, towards the end of which he was made Controller-General of Merchant Shipbuilding in the United Kingdom. He was made first Honorary Freeman of the City of Belfast in 1898, created Baron Pirrie in 1906, and became Knight of the Most Illustrious Order of the Knights of St Patrick two years later. In 1879 he married Margaret Montgomery (niece of Alexander Montgomery Carlisle, senior ship designer at Harland & Wolff). The couple had no children.

Pirrie seems the very embodiment of Yeats's 'smiling public man' and by all accounts was an irresistible salesman who secured orders for ships even from those who didn't want them or need them. Yet W. T. Stead, the famous contemporary journalist, social campaigner and spiritualist, saw Pirrie as unfathomable: 'those who knew him best say they knew him least' as he carved his way to fame and fortune 'in comparative solitude of soul'. Despite the past tense, Stead published his admiring 'Character Sketch' of Pirrie in his *Review of Reviews* in March 1912 and remarked on Pirrie's recent and successful operation (perhaps for prostate cancer). In it he called Pirrie's shipyard 'the greatest business of the kind that has existed in the world since men began to go down to the sea in ships'. A month later, Stead walked up the gangplank on to *Titanic* (as Pirrie couldn't, due to his illness) but reached no earthly destination. From the other side, however, Stead communicated his drowning on the stricken ship and its aftermath, and Sir Arthur Conan Doyle saw the 1913 book of Stead's communications to mediums as furnishing 'enormous' evidence for the occurrence of posthumous messages after accidents at sea. In 1922 Stead's daughter published *The Blue Island*, the complete narrative of her father's passage on *Titanic* to beyond the veil. Stead, a hymn-enthusiast, posthumously took credit for suggesting that the band play 'Nearer, My God, to Thee' as the ship went down. What Pirrie might have thought of the story his journalist-admirer 'filed' soon after the 'Sketch' I don't know.

Notes

Cable from James Montgomery, New York, to James Moore, Belfast, 19th April 1912: *Interview Titanic's officers. All unanimous Andrews heroic unto death, thinking only safety others.* Quoted by Shan Bullock, *Thomas Andrews, Shipbuilder* (1912).

'Oh Tommie, Tommie Andrews we are all so proud of you': co-written by Dr W. F. N. O'Loughlin, Senior Surgeon, White Star Line. The doctor, born in Ireland, did not survive the sinking. The purser of RMS *Oceanic* in 1907 and 1909 (and later of RMS *Olympic*) was C. B. Lancaster, perhaps O'Loughlin's co-songwriter. The song was sung to the tune of the refrain of 'Private Tommy Atkins' of which there is a venerable recording by Robert Howe on YouTube.

'A Queen's Island Trojan, he worked to the last . . .' From a poem by Thomas Carnduff (1886–1956), known as The Island Poet (from the Queen's Island, site of Harland & Wolff) and The Shipyard Poet.

'that priest chap': Fr Frank Browne, Society of Jesus (1880–1960), who sailed on *Titanic* from Southampton but on the orders of his Provincial Superior in Dublin disembarked at Cobh, Ireland. Browne later joked that it was the only time Holy Obedience saved a man's life. He was a prolific photographer and captured life on board the liner, but after the sinking he incurred the displeasure of Harland & Wolff when he wished to give illustrated lectures on the historic event. He served with distinction as chaplain to the Irish Guards during the Great War. He travelled widely thereafter and compiled an impressive portfolio of photographs of exotic places.

'they could receive no severer punishment . . .': Dr Charles H.
Parkhurst, from the pulpit of the Madison Square Presbyterian
Church, 21st April, 1912.

'Forsooth! The very name of the ship breathed the spirit of human
self-conceit . . .': Rev. John Pollock, St Enoch's Presbyterian
Church, Belfast, 21st April, 1912.

'Let me but do my work from day today . . .': from a sonnet by
Henry van Dyke Jr (1852–1933), American author, professor of
English and Presbyterian minister. 'Work' appeared in *Music and
Other Poems* (1904).

Ardara: the Andrews family home in Comber, County Down. In
its garden the young Tommie kept the same number of hives as W.
B. Yeats daydreamed for himself when he would retreat to the Lake
Isle of Innisfree: nine.

'Belfast has beaten the proudest cities of the Empire . . .': These
'local pride' claims for Belfast are properly attributable to Thomas,
Lord O'Hagan (1815–1885), Belfast lawyer, newspaper editor,
campaigner in his early career for repeal of the Act of Union and
first Roman Catholic Lord Chancellor of Ireland: 'Is it a vain
boast to say that Belfast has outrun in the race of progress many of
the proudest cities of the Empire, and exhibited to the world the
spectacle of an Irish community, aided by no physical advantages,
trusting to no adventitious support, fostered by no patronage of
Cabinets or Parliaments, pampered by no doles from the treasury
of the State, by its own inherent energy and determined purpose,
exalting itself to industrial eminence and social importance with
a speed almost unparalleled and a success beyond expectation or
belief?'

'I chose John Kempster instead . . .': John Westbeech Kempster served as President of the Belfast Association of Engineers. Later he was the author of *Britain's Financial Plight, a Review of the Country's Finances* (1928) and *Banking, Credit and the Crisis* (1932). A man of considerable versatility, in September 1914 he addressed the Ulster Liberal Association on 'The Great Conflict between Right and Might' (published in New York and Belfast).

Bram Stoker, 'The World's Greatest Ship-Building Yard', *The World's Work* (UK), 54 (May 1907): 647–50.